The Story of an Old Centerfold

The Story of an Old Centerfold

As Told by

Kristinea

Charleston, SC
www.PalmettoPublishing.com

The Story of an Old Centerfold

Copyright © 2021 by Kristinea

All rights reserved.

No portion of this book may be reproduced, stored in a retrieval system, or transmitted in any form by any means–electronic, mechanical, photocopy, recording, or other–except for brief quotations in printed reviews, without prior permission of the author.

First Edition

Paperback ISBN: 978-1-63837-800-6

In loving memory of my Father…my Dad, my friend, my Marine, and in loving memory of Joplin… my Baby, my pal, my shadow, my Bobby McGee; she was so much more than just my dog, but that is for another story.

Also, to my loving husband Dennis, thank you for supporting me through this journey…"Who's your bitch?" *(inside joke)*

I want to thank my Babes; *you know who you are.* You are one damn beautiful woman… smart, and so much fun to be around. I thank you for all your help.

Music is my escape.
Music is my friend.
Music is my reality.

Chapter One

Growing up in the 80's, 90's sure the hell was a lot of fun, in some ways. I come from a divorced family. My Mom worked hard all her life to provide for all us kids, 4 of us. Dad was always unavailable I guess you could say. He was an alcoholic, traveled on the road awhile, finally coming home when I was 16 years old. Ha! I immediately left my Mom's and went to go live with my Dad. I wanted to be with my Father for many reasons. I wanted to get to know him. I always thought I was left out when I would see my friends' families all together. Also, because I wanted to know the man that would write me a Birthday card and Christmas card; I would get one every year from the time I can remember, about seven years old or so. I wanted someone I could look up to. He had a very good job at a manufacturing company. He was there for over 25 years.

I was only 17 years old, I felt free because my Mom had no idea that my Brother and I, Gordy, used to party with a lot of pot!! She had no clue; I still laugh about it today because it is a great memory

Kristinea

when we get on the subject of Gordy. But every teenager feels that way when they are young, free, invincible, and now my Dad is home. That's how I felt anyway, no more bullshit. No more watching my Mom getting hit by a man because she wouldn't do this or do that. No more not knowing where we were going to lay our heads, because it was hard for her to support us. She did turn to a couple of men, and they did her wrong. And I had to watch it, feeling absolutely helpless. All I ever wanted growing up, was my Dad. And now I got what I wanted. He was home. He was My Dad.

We lived in a one-bedroom apartment behind a grocery store. Sometimes he would sleep in the bedroom, and I would sleep on the couch or vice versa. He worked first shift, I worked 2nd shift at a manufacturing company in town. I hated it. I was only making somewhere around $3.25, it was a temp-to-hire deal though, and I absolutely hated it. Well, of course my checks where small, shit; when your young and come from nothing, you want nice things, that is how I felt. I didn't last long at this company; not long at all. But Dad knew I was out drinking and smoking pot, he wasn't stupid.

The Story of an Old Centerfold

He sat me down one day and said, "Bean, stay with this company, they will take you far in life, give it a try. Yeah, I know you want this, and I know you want that, it will come in time. Don't leave this company Bean. I mean it. I don't want to hear that you quit your job. You are going to be 18 years old soon, and we need extra money. I'm asking you," as he opened his can of beer and smoked his cigarette.

Like many nights, he would open several more, cook dinner and we would have great talks through-out the night. Then we would go to sleep. I would always say, "Dad, sleep in the bedroom, I'll take the couch." I knew he worked harder than I did that day and he deserved to have a good night's rest. Also, I had to think of a way to make more money than I was making. I had to come up with a plan. I had no idea, it was right in front of my nose, from some people that know me; I just didn't realize it. Well, back in the day, damn, I feel so old saying that!

Kristinea

I had a friend "J", that owned a bar. Shit, a few of us from high school would go to the bar. Got in free, free drinks, you name it, they had it or they would get ahold of it. Ha! *Love you J*. If you're reading this!! I was introduced to a new world after I met my friend J, and another guy.

Well, when I say new world, it was. I wasn't a bad looking girl growing up. I was always compared to a model, mainly Cindy Crawford. I was asked "Hey, ya want to make some real money? You're almost 18 years old, no law against it." I thought for a minute one night at the bar, Stripper AKA Entertainer. HMMMM...I said, "Sure. I'm not 18 years old yet J, but I can tell my Dad that I got requested to over-time at work, into some early mornings".

"You going to buy me some things, outfits, etc.? I got to have booze to get up there and do this, ya know." "Why?" he said, "You do the Wet T-Shirt Contest here and you win it almost every time. By the way, people are bitching at me about that." "What do you mean? I get to drink here, I'm under-age, you know that. It isn't my fault I look better than others."(Yeah, I was conceded, and I still feel I have that right. I'm 45 years old, every wrinkle I have I have gained that right to have them. Yeah, I got a few gray hairs, yep, I have gained them too, I have even gained some

The Story of an Old Centerfold

weight. That sucks HA! That's what My Punching Bag is for HA!) SO, I SAID FUCK IT!

I got some outfits and about a week later, I started. I can remember the first time on stage. I was shaking like crazy. I had no Idea what I was doing. I had very little booze in my body, and it sucked ass!! The only thing that made it good was to meet a partner in crime. What I mean by that, is a very beautiful woman. She and I liked the same music, so they put us on stage together. We rocked out to some awesome tunes and took our tops off and got paid for it. She would also get me booze because she was older than me and well, she could get away with anything, just because of the way she looked. Very lean, tall, beautiful body, no boobs though. HAHA!! I mean nothing, I used to tell her to go pop her blackheads on her tits when we would get all drunk and rowdy. That was us. It always takes two to tango. We were meant to be up on stage together. We got the guys all rowdy and yelling and throwing money at us. We were the Bomb that hit the industry. Chante and Kristinea.

We stayed mainly in Iowa, but we would travel to different places together and she later, came to be my roommate for a couple years. I can remember one night, I let her borrow an outfit, she was so drunk. She put it on backwards, OH SHIT…Men were all over the stage giving her money like it was falling from a waterfall, while I'm getting no attention; she was. Well, I danced up towards her, and just busted out laughing. I pulled her aside and said, "Chante Your Pussy is Showing!" The music was stopped, we picked up all the money, got off stage and were sent to the back, where we would get dressed. We got an ass chewing session from the owner. HAHA!! You just had to be there, or at least a fly on the wall. It is a memory that will stay with me forever, that night. I think she walked out with seven hundred that night and I walked out with about three hundred. She always made more than me. I didn't get jealous. She deserved every penny of it. She was a hustler too; I wasn't.

I was just there for the money and booze and all the laughs we had together. This went on for quite some time before my Dad found out. I remember that day as well. I had saved up enough money and went and got me a little white Pontiac Fiero. I loved that car. I was stupid. One day, I went home and left the chest I had kept locked up in the front seat: not even paying attention, careless. It had all my stripper clothes in it. I could have tried to put it in the back, But I didn't try, and I don't think it would have fit anyway. Well, my Dad went to the grocery store, came home very upset.

"BEAN!" I heard him scream, "Get in the kitchen, we need to talk!" "Oh shit!" I said to myself, "He knows, I can feel it, and I can hear it in his tone of voice." I got done taking a shower after rock climbing and cleaning up. I went and sat down at the kitchen table. My heart was pounding, and I was shaking like crazy. And I was scared, I knew my Dad would never hit me, or kick me out, I just knew he was a pissed off Marine and knew that I was in trouble.

"Do you want to show me a check stub from work and the hours you been working?" "Dad, I dropped all that off at Mom's because she holds on to those things for me, because you know how I am! I lose things."

"Okay, who's white Fiero is out there?" "It's mine Dad, I bought it!" I said with a big smile on my face, not remembering what was in the front seat. "Okay, BEAN what's in the front seat? Don't lie to me, I was a trucker for a while, you know that right?"

The Story of an Old Centerfold

"Yes, Dad I know. It's my chest filled with strip clothes. Dad, I've been stripping. I make a lot of money Dad. A lot of money compared to what I would make at the factory."

I could see the disappointment, and a little laughter in his eyes. He told me "BEAN, I guess if I looked like you and had tits and an ass, I would do the same thing. But YOU GOT TO BE CAREFUL! And another thing, save your money, buy some rental properties, or apartments. Invest in something if you're going to live in this apartment. This is what you want to do to make money, INVEST BEAN, INVEST, you will thank me later." I wish I would have listened to my Dad years ago, I'd be better off, that's for damn sure.

My relationship with my Dad grew stronger every day. We became Father and Daughter and best friends.

I got pregnant at a young age; 18 Years old. I stripped for about 4 months. I didn't really show, except my boobs and it made me make more money. My first-born girl. Her Father and I got married basically to give her a name. He has and always will be a dead beat father to me. He was never around. He was partying when I was working 12-hour shifts, taking my clothes off to support us all. The only thing I can say about this man or piece of shit is what I call him, is he went to my Dad and asked for my hand in marriage. That is the only thing I respect him for. The rest was hell.

Shortly before that, Chante came to live with us, and she stayed with us. A friend of the dead beat, the dead beat, and I, and a baby growing in my stomach. I couldn't do my job without some substance in me. So, I smoked a little weed, occasionally, not all the time. It sucked going up on stage, no one knew I was pregnant. But when the tits started to leak milk, I had to stop. I did one last gig for the Four H Club; I think it was called. I made a lot of money. I thought it was a lot anyway. And my Daughter was born two weeks after my 19th Birthday.

    My Mom helped me a lot, she knew I had to go to work, and she knew what I did. She was pissed, she didn't take it like my Dad did. She wasn't happy, but I asked her, "Are you going to pay my bills?" And that was that. When I wasn't working, I raised my daughter, for 16 years, that situation will come later, of what happened to us. I stripped for about 4 years, and I have nothing to show for it. Absolutely nothing.

    Like I said, if I would have listened to my Dad, I would be better off, but I was young and dumb. I was in my 3rd year of stripping, and I had a regular that came in and seen me. He brought in a magazine with him that last time I seen him, he was moving out of state. He handed it to me and said, "Get in this, you will win, I know you will.

    " OH, OKAY, I don't know if I could do that." " You're not doing anything different than you are now! Everyone will see your beauty." I kind a thought Okay…well…maybe… I never seen him again. But the thought of that Men's Magazine and winning the Top Prize, never left my mind.

    After all, Chante was also in a popular men's magazine, Lingerie Edition. I had seen it one time; it was beautiful. She was "The Shit" In my eyes; the most beautiful woman you could ever see. No Joke! Let your imagination take this, tall, lean, nice ass to twerk with, but no damn boobs…but it didn't matter. Every man she met, she put some sort of spell on them, I think it was fantasy. She made the book, she made a lot of money as well, but she deserved every penny of it. She

The Story of an Old Centerfold

rocked the house down like no woman I have ever met, and she and I together were "The Shit." We didn't really do anything pole dancing, but I had the tits, she had the ass, I was all legs, and we both looked good. That's for damn sure. We would rock out to ZZ top, Alice in Chains, and the Doors. We sometimes would have to make it quick, because you've got to look absolutely fabulous, when you come to stage, so if we were scheduled early, we wouldn't give a fuck. We would make it count later in our scheduled times to dance.

We strippers were the worst; at least some of us anyway. Always, lock your shit…make up, outfits, money, everything you own at that moment, lock it up! Girls would steal from your ass. Always be in lockdown or have a good friend that would watch your stuff.

The outfits and the music had to fit, or no damn money. And Chante and I went through a lot of shit together. She would watch mine and I would watch hers. That's how we dealt, and anybody that fucked with us, we always had each other, no matter what. But Damn, what a woman in my eyes. Very independent, beautiful, smart, nice body and a lot of class; a lot of class. Our nights usually didn't start out 'til about 9 PM. That's when we would have most fun, boozed up, and ready to Rock the Club down to the ground. Before I got pregnant, she came to live with us for about two years. It was good times and bad times.

She got into a car wreck one night because she couldn't handle all the fighting between dead beat and I, so she left. She was at a red stop light with the other traffic going with a yellow light. This was about 2:00 AM in the morning. She was hit on the left side of her car, by a man that was at the bar we had danced at all day and night. Police came, she was intoxicated, and then an ambulance.

She was let off. She came home around 3:30 that morning. I stayed awake and waited for her. I was worried about her, at the time and for a long time she was my best friend.

She gets home and tells me and him to stop fighting, her car is totaled, and I hear in the background the ambulance man, "Please let me take care of you, you don't have to do this kind of work anymore." I will basically kiss your ass anytime you want," is what he was saying, and it was because of her beauty. Those gorgeous eyes, they could mesmerize anybody. Especially men, young and old. She continued to live with us for about two years. She spent all her money investing into stocks, like I was told to do but didn't. She invested a lot of what she made, we didn't charge her any rent or money for food. Dead beat dad's roommate was so in love with her, he would do anything for her. I mean ANYTHING. Plus, I liked having her around. The laughs, the tears, everything we went through more than 90% of the time we went through it together.

Chapter Two

After living with each other for a couple years, Chante went back home. At that time, Dead beat's Father was selling the house, so he and I got our own place. It didn't last but six months, I filed for a divorce. I couldn't stand coming home to a messy place and my baby with shit all up in her diaper, because he was too busy partying and destroying the house and not watching her, or not changing her diaper for I don't know how long. I was still drinking myself, so it was hard.

I continued to count on my Mom. I got my own place, had a Corvette, and continued to strip. I guess I did it so long that I got used to that money and being able to make it on my own. I chose the hours, and clubs and then would be home for two weeks. I had it all, independence, good looking, nice car, and a beautiful girl. I'm not here to say she had the best life because she didn't. I was trying the best I knew how to provide for her and pay my bills. Being a Mom and a Dad at the same time. But as I write this, it was mainly my Mom that

took care of her. I thank her for that, but I'm not happy with the way she turned out. Even as a person and an adult. I'm sure she can say I was a bitch or a mean Mom, and that's okay with me. Because I've learned, what goes around comes around.

But back to Chante and me. She had moved to a bigger city in Iowa. I decided to go down there and dance with her. A lot more girls and a lot more hustling; that just wasn't me. I didn't know how to hustle. I should have learned with her around, but I just didn't fit that image.

I was young and trying to raise a daughter and still be young at the same time. I had her at such a young age, I feel that was taken away from me, SO Yeah, I am a bad Mom. I was a kid having a kid, with no help from anyone but my Mom.

I would stay with Chante in her apartment and things really started to change between us. We were fighting a lot and she was on some hard ass drugs. The bad kind. Meth. It even sounds terrible, the name. I'm not going to sit here and say I was perfect because I wasn't. I liked my cocaine; she liked her meth. She had a beautiful dog, named Ajax. I was cooking breakfast one morning and I wasn't happy with the way the eggs turned out, so I threw them away. I grabbed a glass of orange juice in a blue glass, and the next thing I know, I'm getting yelled at for throwing away my eggs and making new ones and using her favorite glass.

We got into it. Yelling, screaming, all the above, throwing glasses at each other. We just went off on each other. We didn't play around when we started fighting. It was all because of meth. I told her to get off her ass and take her dog out. She'd come back at me and say, "He

The Story of an Old Centerfold

can hold it." It shocked me because she loved that dog, but the meth was more important. I didn't stay there much longer.

I found someone else to travel with and I was making decent money. There were nine or ten of us girls who were supposed to go to Japan to strip at an exclusive club. Everyone backed out except for my travel companion. I told her, "Look, I know you can take care of yourself, but I've decided I'm coming with you." My Mom was not happy about the decision. You didn't hear about sex trafficking in those days; she was worried I wouldn't make it back, but still, she agreed to keep my daughter. I got a ninety day visa, and before I knew it, I was at LAX and heading for Japan.

When we got to Japan, we stayed in an apartment across the street from a grocery store. Below us were what I called *clam shuckers*. Every Sunday, we could see the fireworks from Disneyland. It was amazing. There were only nine of us girls at the club; that made the hustling easy for me. They loved the way I looked because I looked like one of them…I had a tan body and was very tone. This was different dancing. The stage attire was a dress…long, I may add, and gloves over your hands. That or nothing. The stage fee was $130 a night.

I was making $3k a night. We also made money from drink sales. It didn't take long for me to have some regulars. There was one in particular called Fuji. He spoke perfect English. We were told most people in the area could speak English, ah, no they couldn't. Fuji always paid our stage fees.

The down-time was crazy. It was either wait 'til sunset for the subway and go out or we would have parties. What parties we would have! Bars were open all night and clubs were everywhere. My favorite

club had a red door. Metallica would be playing, I'd have $3k in purse and would drink flaming Dr Pepper shots with the fire and all. There were Japanese people singing songs in the English language but knew no meaning of the words. I often wondered, "How the hell do you even know what you're singing?" We would often walk down the road wasted off our asses, and not get in trouble.

After a month, I continued to stay because I was killing it in money; it was a beautiful country as well. I was making more money than my travel companion, and the arguments began. I was one of the main girls - top girl making the cash. One day I had a man in uniform buy me a couple of drinks. He was in the military, a supervisor of a submarine. He was fabulous. I took him to the apartment one night after work. Hey, I was single, and I wasn't scared of the man at all. We went at it all night and damn the man could eat some pussy. My lips were so swollen the next day. I made almost $6k the night after and I came back to the apartment to find a bunch of yellow roses. I mean dozens. My travel companion was so jealous and pissed. She told me, "Good luck finding your way around because I won't ride with you anymore." "Okay," I answered. Besides, it wasn't that hard to find your way around, you just followed the colors on the subway. I went to Tokyo Disneyland, the wax museum and I got to see Buddha. Venturing out on my own, I found my favorite place to eat, The Hard Rock Café. I always got wings and celery to take with me to work. Well, every damn day my boss would come in and say, "Tori!"(*that was my stage name*) "Get your ass out there and get to work!" I'd be in my long dress, eating wings. I would come back at him with, "Fuck off, I'm eating, I've got almost $3k in my purse, I'm fucking eating." "You're fined $500 on your credit card!" he would say. "You think I

The Story of an Old Centerfold

give a shit?" I'd bark back. He would come back and fine me more money and I would just laugh at his skinny ass and say, "Ya know Fuji covers all my fines in American cash. Keep it up and I'll tell him about you." Fuji did pay all my fines and I told him about my boss fining me every day. He asked if I wanted him dead. I said, "Oh, no." Something just didn't seem right in my mind with Fuji, "Who are you?" I asked. "I'm a mafia leader," he answered. I went to get up, and he grabbed my hand gently and said, "Please, sit down Tori." I did sit back down, and he told me the ropes…I found out there were three main mafias in Japan. I was in total shock and scared. At that point, I wanted to go home.

The fines continued, along with me giving my boss the finger. I decided I was going to get even with him one night we all went out. I had been featured in a magazine, promoting the club and my boss got an escort he found in the magazine. We all began to drink we had a lot to drink. I took that girl from him. I handed her $1k, and she came home with me. She was absolutely beautiful. We didn't do anything. I tried to speak and write to communicate with her and got nowhere. She left the next morning. I got bitched out bigtime when I got to work and was fined over $500 because he had already paid for her. Ha! Ha! He did kinda stop fucking with me after that.

One night I was sitting at a table with a bunch of dentists and Fuji was at the head of the table. I got dances from every one of them. At one point while sitting, Fuji was trying to have a conversation with me, and the other men were talking. He made one gesture and said quick words and like that, the entire table was quiet. "What did you say to them?" I asked. "I told them to be quiet, I'm trying to have a conversation with my Tori." The power Fuji had was impressive and scary.

While this was going on my friend was freaking out and bothering me because Dime-bag Darryl was at the club. I didn't care, I was there to make the money and I sure the hell did.

I was still seeing my submarine man, but he was leaving soon. That was a hard goodbye. The money, the partying and constant action was a whirl-wind, one night I saw what was really going on and it all came to a head. We had people outside the club with walkie-talkie headsets, running in all directions, distracting the police and mafia from the club. Nude clubs are supposed to be closed at midnight, not 3 AM. I was sitting with Fuji, and he suddenly wanted a dance. He never once asked me before for one. We went to a back area, and I start to dance. "No Tori, sit down and be quiet!" he said. "What the fuck Fuji?" I asked. He told me that the club owner owed another person and things were about to get very ugly. And it sure the fuck did.

A man came in with a machete looking knife; it was huge. I was crying and we were hunched down hiding. The alarms went off and everyone was on lockdown. I don't know what happened with the man or if the knife was used; it was chaos. After about an hour the place cleared, and Fuji told me he was concerned for my travel companion and for my safety. He handed me a gold key and told me to go to this hotel with my friend. He opened a credit card for me and said he would be in touch. I went shopping like in that classic fairy-tail movie about the call girl who ends up with a billionaire client, but I knew it wasn't good…it wasn't a good situation, and it was time to go home.

The Story of an Old Centerfold

I got on a plane without my friend, my travel companion. Our friendship was over because of this trip and the club. I got screwed out of $10k that was on club credit, but I was leaving with money…$35k.

Flying back to the US, I couldn't wait to get off the plane. I kissed the fucking ground and cried for joy. I felt so safe again. When I got home, I paid my debts, and took a few weeks off to spend time with my little girl.

I was still kinda lost without my best beautiful Goddess, Chante. One night a friend and I were invited to a party at her apartment after work. We went and what I saw was unbelievable. Meth on a plate that looked like a mountain from her friend, "Bitch," is what I like to call him, he looked like he just came out of the fucking gutter and was no saint in my eyes. Bikers all over the place, I trusted them more than that Bitch. Alcohol everywhere, cocaine, pot, you name it, it was there.

I pulled her aside about this gutter guy and said, "What are you doing? Who is this man? Ya know, if we get loud in here, we are all busted." She told me to shut up and he gave her free drugs. I had enough at that point and had a two-hour drive home. I left.

I didn't see or talk to her for a few weeks and went alone to strip joints to work, not an easy thing to do at age 21. Being by myself made it even scarier. Anything could have happened to me; anything.

I went back a few times to the old stomping grounds of where Chante and I had worked together. Seeing her and that nothing had changed there, I just worked alone. I know if anyone had looked in my eyes, they would have seen a lost person.

I became good friends with an older gentleman at one of the clubs I was working at. He was a regular and he was just the sweetest man you could ever meet. On the dead days, he was always there to talk to, about anything.

Finally, Chante and I were speaking again, and she met him, the older gentleman. We were like the 3 musketeers when we were together. We just had fun.

Chapter 3

I met Chante's Gutter Guy, The Bitch, at the club she worked at. She introduced us, he bought me a drink. I talked to him for a bit, and it went from there. I had seen him a few times before and he had dated every stripper in there. I was told about the size of his dick before we were ever together.

I found out what he did for a living, he had cleaned up and wasn't too bad looking. Chante wouldn't give him my number for a while and to this day, I wish she never would have. But I was at home, I had a few weeks off work and about two years after first meeting him, he asked her for my phone number. She called me and asked me if I wanted him to have it, and I said, "Well, today is my birthday and Mom is babysitting, so I guess". He called and we went out that night.

We had a few drinks, he came to my home and never left. That's how the Bitch and I started.

I didn't know how to cook, I always watched my Mom, so we lived off spaghetti for a long time. He met my daughter, and he somewhat became a father figure for her. The tables were turned a little bit. I had a man, that made good money. I stayed home more often, began to spend the much-needed time with my little girl.

After about a year or so of being with him, his grandparents weren't doing too well, so we moved to his hometown out of state. They had a farm and we stayed in the spare house on the property. We had Santa come one year and meet my little girl at the house. I had a German Shepard, beautiful dog he was. I enrolled in college for bookkeeping. We went on a trip and got married in Lake Tahoe. Just him, myself, a witness, and a pastor. Nothing big, he wasn't on drugs because he was back working for the union and life wasn't that bad anymore. I kept in touch with My Dad on a daily basis; no matter where I was or what I was doing. I still had that strong, wise, Marine in my life. I put my stripping items away for a while and it was such a good feeling.

Everything, I thought, seemed to be going well. The house we were living in was abandoned years ago, so it was old. It needed a lot of cleaning. I always loved cleaning because my Mom and I would do it when I was a teenager. I enjoyed it because there was a time where my Mom and I were very close, but not as close as my Dad and me.

I was cleaning the bathroom one day upstairs, I did the best I could, and Bitch was drinking; he got violent with me. Grabbed me by my wrist and drug me in the upstairs bathroom and bitched me out. It was an absolute nightmare. I never seen him like this, and he hit the booze hard, just like I did, and I had quit for some time. But after that happened, he got really physical with my kid. Beating her

The Story of an Old Centerfold

ass all the time, coming after me all the time, just boozed up and a mean Bitch. I did stay with him even after he started hitting my kid all the time. Hey, I was in Love, I loved him; today I hate him and I'm not afraid to say that.

I had to think of a way to stay until my student loans came in and grants. I wanted so badly to finish college. So, I began to pick up this magazine I was told about years earlier. Every month for about 5 months. I began to study it, what I mean by that is look at the images, what they were looking for, long hair, or short hair, short or tall, fake, or real boobs. Then one day I said to myself, "This man has told me I fuck really good, and I got his heart." Well, that's what I did. Fucked him constantly; when he wanted it, he got it, even quickies.

I then brought up the magazine to him. I showed him it a few times and he was like, "Hell Yeah Hun, you can make that." So, it began, him taking a lot of pictures of me, dressed, half dressed and totally nude...Ya know why? I was in a contest for a prominent spot in a popular men's magazine. I fit the image and I knew I did. You were only supposed to send in 5 pictures. Well, I took it further, I sent in about 100 pictures. I took it to the limit because I was on a mission. I wanted to win, damn it!

Before I sent those pictures off, I kissed the envelope and wished for the best. I called every day for a month and spoke with a woman, can't remember her name, just stating, "Hey, this is Kristinea, did you get my pictures?" I sent in a lot because I really want to do this, and I want to win." Every day it was, "Yes, we have, we will be in touch…" Then since I was the squeaky wheel, I got a phone call. I won the July issue of this well-known men's magazine *Girl of The Month*! There were two messages on the voicemail that day. One from this company

Kristinea

telling me I won, and another telling me one of my 3 Musketeers was murdered. My good old pal that Chante met earlier. I was in total shock. The feelings of everything coming at me like a blow to the face and a dream come true. I lost My friend.

My father called and gave me the news, he was on the voicemail. I dropped to my knees in disbelief, because I just had something wonderful happen, and my Friend was murdered. I called My Dad crying in disbelief, and crying tears of happiness, because I won this contest. Dad was happy for me, I told him what the average amount I would be making in about 2 months was going to be, and then I cried for my Friend. I called Chante after I calmed down, had a few glasses of wine, and I didn't think she would answer her phone, but she did that night.

I got on the phone and said, "You're not going to believe this!" "What is going on? "she asked?

"Our 3rd Buddy at the strip club we used to sit and have fun with is dead" She said, "No way." I began to tell her what happened. "He was working night shifts at an adult bookstore and an African American man, just out of prison for two months, came and got him. He stabbed him 73 times, Chante," I was crying my eyes out. She also began to cry, but my mouth got me and cost me our friendship. The only reason being was, I said I wish Iowa had the death penalty, and other things. She hung up on me, told me she was done with me and how dare I say that. That night I realized I lost two people in my life, one from murder and one from whatever words I was saying that night. I was hurting.

I called my Dad a lot just to talk to him, for him to tell me, "Bean, calm down, Bean, it will all work out. Bean you got other things to

The Story of an Old Centerfold

focus on, Bean, I Love You." And having him by my side and telling me this truly got me through all the bullshit. I would call and call my Beautiful Friend and it was busy or she wouldn't answer. I never spoke to her again. As I write this, I don't know where she is, I don't know what happened to her and I don't even know if she still exists. I have tears running down my eyes because like I said before, she was my Buddy, my partner in crime and damn it, I miss her. I have tried over many years to find her, and I have been unsuccessful. So, I've had to move on without her in my life.

The man finally went to trial, and he got a life sentence. I've heard many stories after my Friend passed, and I didn't believe any of them. I knew my Friend. My Dad called me about the sentencing and what this bastard got. Not good enough in my eyes, to this day. I did go to my Friend's funeral. It was a hard day; I remembered a lot of the fun times we all had together, and I just was an emotional wreck. I really was. To the point, where I was in disbelief still. Someone he worked with had to hold me back because I wanted to see his body. I wanted to see where he was stabbed 73 times, I wanted to rip his shirt off and just pray that I heard a heartbeat. I knew it wasn't there. But I just wanted to hug him and tell him, thank you for all you did for me. I did hug him, with all the tears running down my face.

When it was over, I had to hop on an airplane shortly after...My destination... The Big Apple, New York City! I'd never been there before; I didn't know what to expect. I packed some real cute clothes that looked good on me too, just in case they didn't have anything.

Chapter 4

When I got off the plane, I had a classy car waiting for me and an usher and a security guard. I felt like someone high class. I met everyone in the company, their positions, and what I would be doing. Which was eating whatever I wanted, high dollar, food, fine dining restaurants and fine wine. Next was taking a photo shoot. I met the guy that did my first shoot. In my eyes, he was unprofessional. Very rude and I just didn't feel comfortable. So, they put me in an Uncle Sam outfit, and the photo shoot began. If anyone has that issue you can tell I was very uncomfortable with him; I only smiled a few times.

    I made the cover of a well-known men's magazine's *Girl of The Month*, for July. They even made posters of the cover. I only have one left in my home, that is it. Those are very hard to come across these days, shit I was only 22 when I got in the magazine, and I'm not going to lie but the man that owned this company was one hot, older Italian man and damn he had one hell of a body, and big hands. I love big hands. I could just sit and dream about this man and look at him.

The Story of an Old Centerfold

That's exactly what I did, dream and look, and sometimes I would get so turned on by him I would masturbate by myself and think of him. I know it sounds crazy, but I did. I was a married woman, and I couldn't cheat, it wasn't in my blood. And I was in love with my husband.

Anyway, I got bitched out a few times by my photographer and I flat out told his ass, "Look here buddy, this is way different than taking my clothes off in front of my husband and him taking the pictures." After all, there was only a few of us there. I knew I was safe, but I was extremely uncomfortable. I asked for some champagne to calm me down a little.

The photographer said, "Get her something to drink or we are going to be here 'til midnight and I got shit to do." So, they did; it loosened me up a little and the photoshoot ended early enough so this asshole didn't have to be around me, and I didn't have to be around him much longer. I was thankful it was finished. It turned out Okay, but I know it could have been better. I was born to be in front of a camera, it loved me, and I loved it. I then did a few radio station interviews and got to meet some really nice people. That was the best part to start off this journey and I was getting paid a lot of money to do it. Shit, even the Bitch got paid because he took the pictures. It was a win-win situation. After being in New York for a few days, it was time to go home. I received the issue in the mail, along with some black and white pictures of me dressed, that didn't look to bad. I honestly thought if I had a better down to earth photographer, it would have turned out better, but it wasn't good and it wasn't bad, if that makes any sense.

I was told they would be in touch, and I was up for winning *Girl of The Year* for 1999. I knew this was a contest and the best would win.

Kristinea

I had a fucking poster of myself, holy shit that feeling of seeing yourself on a poster was like, "Holy Shit, Kristinea, you're in; your foot is in the door, and you made a good impression the first time, so you may have this!" I bought the magazine every month just to see who I was fighting against, there were a few that I thought oh shit, she's going to get it for this reason, or this girl is going to get it because of this. By this time, I had finished my degree in bookkeeping. I graduated with a Grateful Dead Hat on at the ceremony.

My name was on a marquis outside of a lingerie shop, in the town we were living in. I did a book signing there and it was packed. Almost a block of men down the road wanting to meet me and get their book signed by me.

The Story of an Old Centerfold

It was great to feel that way, knowing that I did this by myself, and the men loved everything about me. I was bubbly, I was pretty, I always had a smile on my face, and I had a lot of fun.

I had the guys going, just like I did in the clubs. Accept, I was missing someone. My friend, my Beautiful Goddess. I thought about her a lot during that time; I still do. I mean shit, she was in a prominent magazine and here, I was too. How did that happen? I still question myself about it, but I think it had a lot to do with being in the right place at the right time. For some reason, I had the look, the *Girl of The Month* look; it fit me well, I may add. The Bitch and I decided to leave the state and come back to Iowa. We lived in a nice house by a well-known lake in Iowa. I loved it out there, it was quiet and so peaceful. I would see so many deer come up to the window and eat the corn and lick the salt blocks the Bitch went out and bought. He was on the road working and I was at home. I slowly began to learn how to cook. We were a family. I had the world by the ass and so did the Bitch. But the beatings continued after we moved. The Bitch's favorite drink was orange juice, vodka, and cranberry juice. Gosh he would hit it hard when he returned from work. I was constantly getting choked and slammed up against the wall or whatever was around me.

He never hit me, it was choking and turning me blue, and then letting go and watching me suffer to get to breathing again. He had a co-worker that I thought wasn't bad looking. We invited him over to the house. Well, that was a shitty idea. We cooked out that day on top of our porch looking out at the lake. It was a beautiful day outside. It was Lee, my daughter, the Bitch, and me. Well, we got to drinking, a lot of drinking. His friend asked me if he could fuck me, I was stupid and very intoxicated and said ask my husband. He did. And we fucked, fucked really hard, soft, sweet, looked at each other in the eyes knowing we were sinning. This man could go and go, and I had a lot of energy and drunk off my ass as well. The Bitch got his jollies off by watching us. It turned him on so much, but we weren't finished for quite some time. We were laughing, rolling around and going after each other like we already knew each other and knew what we both were wanting. It was like we could see in each other, by the looks we made to each other, and damn what a big cock he had.

It was very pleasing, until, Bitch grabbed me, took me out on the porch and tried so hard to fuck me the way his co-worker did. Yeah, he had the sloppy seconds, and for once I didn't give a shit, what he thought, or his feelings, nothing…I didn't care for once. When I say once, I mean it. It took him awhile, and he finally got off. I got up and took a shower. I kinda felt nasty, cruel, and mean for not giving a shit what he thought or what I did with his friend. I went to bed. I woke up cooked everyone breakfast and went downstairs to start a load of laundry.

When Lee came down to the basement, things went to shit again. He whispered in my ear, so soft, sweet, and sexy, "I want to do this again, when he isn't around." I told him, "No, that was a one-time deal, and we had a lot of booze. I'm married, and I cannot do that again." I had no idea Bitch was listening through the vent upstairs. I told him No a few times and he finally gave up, gave his phone number on his business card, handed to me, and said, "When you're sick of the shit, call me, I will take care of you and your daughter better than this asshole does." I took the card and just set it on the washer, it was going to fall off anyway.

The Story of an Old Centerfold

So, we all said goodbye and it started, again. I walked in the house, he grabbed me again, and choked me 'til I was blue. Telling me I'm a whore and I got such a tight pussy all his friends and co-workers wanted me and wanted a piece of me because I was everyone's fantasy, I was a nude model, and that is all I would ever be. He was sober this time. I was a little shocked, but not really. I knew deep down I was going to get it, whether or not, what had happened that night. I could feel it, I knew it was coming. I turned blue again, fighting to breathe, as my daughter watched every time, he had the chance, he made sure she was around. It was bad, the more aggressive he got, I'm surprised I'm still here, he could have killed me many times, but he didn't. He killed my heart, he killed the bubbly girl inside me, he killed me because I didn't want my daughter to see it. He just killed my soul. And it continued for years to come. He left for work, and I was thankful. I felt so at peace when he was on the road. I slowly became myself again, it took a long time, and he would be gone for months at a time. I wasn't fully healed from all the abuse, and as I write this, I am reliving what I went through. Again, but I am safe right now and No Man will ever put his hands on me again. No man. I will live in my car before I another man will touch me.

By this time, I had gotten the phone call I was in the top 5. I called Dad and told him I made the top 5, he said, "Shit Bean, that's how much if you win?" " $25K Dad, $25K and traveling for a year and a half." "Well, I hope you get it, and I hope you invest with the money you receive Bean, do it this time." I then decided if I won, I was going to listen to My Dad and invest. I then got the call, I won. I fucking won. The feeling was something I can't describe in words…

Kristinea

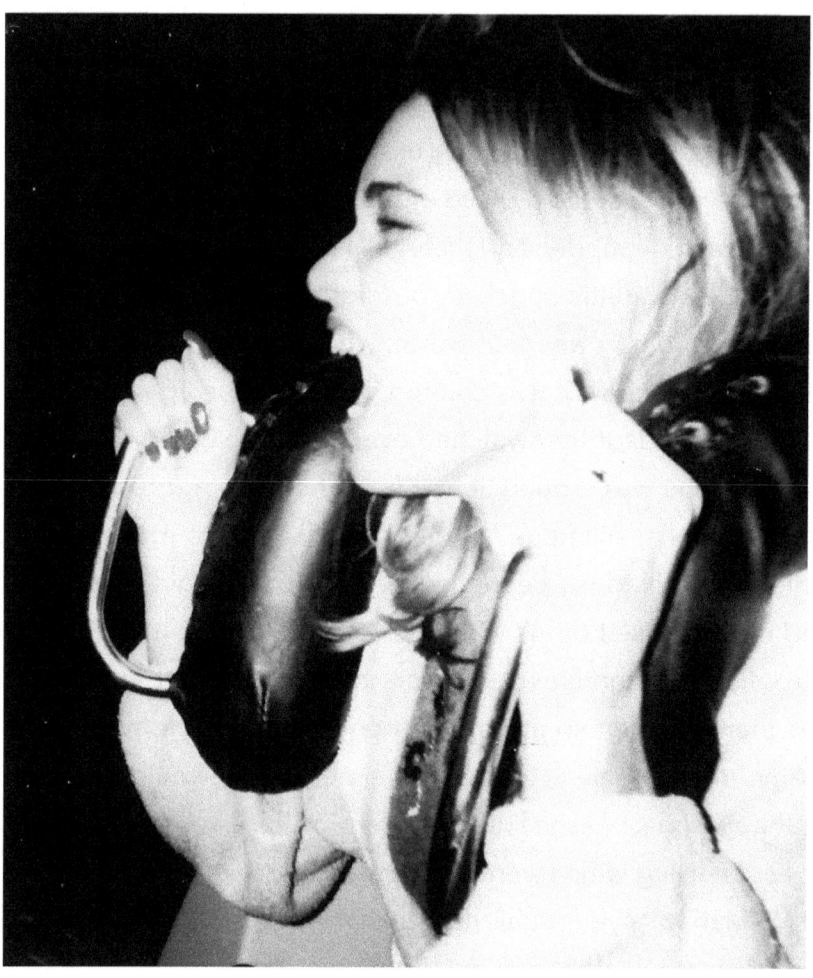

I fucking did it! I got it!!! Holy Shit! It really brought out the self-esteem I was needing at the time. I was just speechless and extremely excited. I thought of my friend that was killed, I couldn't call and tell him, and I always thought of my Beautiful Goddess. I wanted to share it with her and try to get some tips on what to do for the shoot. But, by this time, her number was changed. No more information.

Chapter 5

I got another call everyone was on speaker phone telling me "Congrats!" and "Are you ready for your shoot?" I said, "Well, ya know I'm very excited and I'm ready, but who is doing the photo shoot?" "A different guy this time for you; we knew how you felt the last time and we want some good shots this time. You're going to Marina Del Ray in California. This guy is one of the best in the business. I said, "Oh My God!!" "We are going to be shooting in a mansion that we rented for the weekend." They told me to get ready, pack my clothes, no husband, and no kids allowed. I said, "Okay." I hung up the phone and just screamed!! And then I thought, "Oh shit, I get to see that handsome man again!" And yes, his hands were big as well HAHA!!

So, a week later I was heading to Cali…with a stop in New York first, to receive my sash and a glass of champagne with the company. We got to California and oh, what a beautiful place. I was totally mesmerized by the looks of this place. It was beautiful. I was always met

with a classy car, an usher, and a security guard; everywhere I went. I felt safe, and damn, did I ever feel sexy. The shoot was the next day, I ordered room service, with cheese I never tasted in my life, crackers, and some wine, the finest wine. It was on the house, so I thought well shit Bean, Live it Up and I sure the hell did.

My shoot was a long day and I'm going to say it wasn't easy. Not easy at all. Staying in one place for over 5 minutes, trying not to close my eyes when the sun would shine on my face, and I brought some more clothes and they looked fabulous on me. My Photographer was the best. "You're awesome; You're beautiful; Give it to me… Yeah, there ya go; Give me more…Give me more…The camera loves you sweetie, Love it back…" And that is exactly what I did. I did so much, the pictures were unbelievable. I couldn't believe it was me, I looked damn good, and it showed. I worked so hard that day, and it paid off. Yeah, it paid me $25K Off!!

A few of us went to dinner that night, fresh seafood, the ocean, and just the moonlight would turn anybody on. I went to my hotel and went to bed. I woke up the next morning and I was in pain. I felt like I worked out all day during that shoot. I was always working out in high school and rock climbing, but damn it's been a while. I can even feel it now, that feeling I had. I woke up and the phone rang. The only people that knew I was there was the crew and the Bitch and my Dad. It was the handsome Italian man, saying, "Good Morning; Beautiful shoot we had yesterday." I said, "Thank you, I'm in a lot of pain," and chuckled like a little child. He said, "Yeah, I forgot to tell ya that with this guy, you are going to be in pain, he works ya and you worked it yesterday. I can tell ya that much," and we both laughed.

The Story of an Old Centerfold

He asked me to meet him downstairs for breakfast, always on the house. I got cleaned up still in pain, muscles where hurting like a son of a bitch. I got to the table and got me a bloody Mary, to kind of relax and relieve my pain. There were beautiful flowers at the table. He told me, "These are for you, they aren't decorations." "Okay," I said, and opened the envelope. It said, "Good Morning beautiful Kristinea, I never got you flowers, and I wanted to say Congrats, and welcome to The Magazine. Get ready to travel because we will be going places together. Oh, and here is your first check my dear." Inside was a $5K check and one picture of me. The one they chose to use in the contest.

My very first picture that got me in the contest. I said, "Thank You, that is very thoughtful." We continued to talk about everything I was going to be doing, where I could go with this company and where I couldn't. They had rules. No stripping, no braces, no hair color changing, no gaining weight, no boob jobs, no nothing. Basically, telling me I had to stay the same way I was from the day they first met me. If I were caught stripping, I would be fired; my title would then go to the runner up of the contest, but I didn't worry about that. I hadn't been stripping anyway. It was a long breakfast and I just looked and listened, damn those hands and that tan and oh my how he would light his cigar; that was enough for me to handle. I handled it well I may add but damn I knew I had to get back to my room and just relax a little.

After about 3 hours, I went back up to my room. I laid down in a king size bed, looking at the ocean from my window, and I just got in the mood, I guess. I brought my special little friend with me. My Bullet. And I couldn't help myself, I masturbated again and again and again, multiple orgasms. I took my hand, and went through my hair,

touched my boobs like crazy, licked them and thought of that man. I wore myself out. HAHA! I didn't care, I had to please myself after sitting with a man so powerful and so direct. And that voice, oh my, the voice, I kinda remember it as I write this.

    I slept for a few hours, woke up called my Dad first. I got a check Dad!! $5k Dad!! He was happy for me, asked me about the shoot and how it went and to invest Bean, invest. I then called my Bitch of a husband, told him how it went and hung up. He was at work anyway and Dad had my daughter at the lake house, babysitting. I gave him a beautiful wolf stein with a $100 bill in it for babysitting and he had plenty of beer in the fridge. I made sure he was set for the time I was going to be gone. Only the best for my Dad and my Marine. My Dad was happy for me; my Mom was the one that was pissed off when I first entered. She stayed pissed off too, for a long time. I did some radio interviews and got paid to do it. It was a good time, many laughs, and very nice people to be around in that area of California. I then went home. I was home for about 2 weeks out of every month for a year and a half.

    My next trip was back to the Big Apple to meet everyone I could possibly meet. When I got there, it was top notch, again everything on the house. This was at an Italian restaurant, my favorite. There were magazine distributors there. They all wanted to meet me and to travel to their states. I was so silent at first, but then I loosened up a little bit, thanks to the bartender. He gave me a big wine glass with a shot of Rumple Minze, and a single coffee bean in it. I asked him, "Why the coffee bean?" He replied, "It's for good luck, Beautiful." "Oh, Okay, thank you, never heard of that before." I drank to the good luck, and I got to meet so many people and had so many conversations. Do you

The Story of an Old Centerfold

want to come to Florida? Do you want to come to Alabama? Do you want to come to Kansas? Even Vancouver and the surrounding areas were there. I said yes to every one of them. All I had to do was show up, look good, sign My Centerfold, smile, look happy, which I was.

I was making some good money and wanting to invest, like I decided to. I didn't know much about stocks, but the Bitch had many and he knew a little bit. I spent a few days there and returned home. I received another check by mail, $5K. I sat down with The Bitch and told him I was going to invests this money. He told me, "NO, YOU'RE NOT! We want to put money in the house; we talked about this." "Well, I changed my mind," I said. He went on another anger rage and choked me again, this time leaving fingerprint bruises. I was thankful it was wintertime. I could wear turtlenecks and cover what I could with makeup, but that would come off after some time. I couldn't breathe again, same shit different day and at different times, while my daughter watched. As I write this I cry. She didn't need to see that, and he would continue to beat on her as well. It never stopped. We drank a lot and anything I did or didn't do, would trigger it and it was constant. It was always my fault. Always. I would provoke the beatings. That's what he told me and that's what I believed for many years.

Yeah, I was stupid, more than a box of rocks. I had many travels ahead of me. My favorite places were Canada, Panama City Beach, Florida, Mobile, Alabama, Las Vegas and where I was born and raised in Iowa. I was ready to get away, I feel bad saying that because I had a daughter at home, but I thought, this would be a good way out of this shit we were both putting up with. I was wrong. He actually threatened to kill me when I won this contest. I was specifically told, "If I catch you fucking around on me, I will put you, feet first in a woodchipper, alive by the way." He told me that he could get the equipment from work, and no one would know because his Dad was a big shot. He could get away with anything because of his position at work and he could do nothing or no wrong in everybody's eyes.

I called my Marine, my Dad. I told him what the Bitch told me. I cried and said, "I'm scared Dad, what do I do?" My Dad was silent, he was kinda shocked I wasn't telling him any of this. He told me, "He provides for you and your little one; I can't see him doing this. If he does, we'll call the police. Then I called my Mom. She didn't even know what was going on. I tried to keep it very private, I didn't really have anyone I could talk to. I always had my Dad, but I never really told him, because he could see no wrong in him either, because of the way he provided for all of us. I had everything I could ever ask for and I wasn't happy, but I was still in love. I know a lot of people are

The Story of an Old Centerfold

reading this and understand and I know some of you will say, "Why?" Well, you picked up this book for a reason.

My Mom or my Dad would watch my daughter when I would leave the lake house, I always paid my Dad, I knew he was suffering in many ways, from being in Vietnam. I could see it in his eyes, by his shakes and then what I'd see later on, in our years together. I never paid my Mom, she was working and taking care of my daughter when I wasn't home. I made my schedule, so it would work out to where he wouldn't be home when I was gone, and one of my parents would be there to make sure she was safe. I had to ask for that before I signed all the paperwork, I think they finally found out after my trip to Canada.

My Canada trip....wow...what a beautiful place. I was escorted by police and a magazine distributor. I can't remember this guy's name, but we had fun. Especially, on the plane to get there. I wasn't planning on drinking on the plane, but we did, and we got wasted off our ass. I had a teddy bear; I bought one everywhere I went. So far, this was my favorite one. He asked me, "Why do you do that… buy a teddy bear everywhere you go?" "So, I can have a memory of everywhere I've went and look at it and talk about how much fun I had here or there." He said, "Oh okay, I guess I get it." "I'm a man," he said. You just had to be a fly on the wall or a passenger on that plane that day. He even put Teddy in the seat with a belt.

We finally got there in the evening, and I was in total shock at this place we were staying. It was absolutely beautiful. It looked like apartments, fancy ones but they were just hotel rooms. Beautiful! I tried to look the place up later, but I don't remember, it may possibly be out of business. I went to the biggest mall though, out of the country; that was a blast. I did a few book signings. That's when I had

my fingerprint bruises. The people with me, opened the doors, I seen beautiful red roses everywhere, a banner with my name "Kristinea... Welcome"...and men lined up like crazy to meet me. There was one specific man I remember the most. I signed for a few hours and did a radio station interview at the same time. I would always sign different things. My favorite was this CUN HVN...(*Can You Figure That one out?*)....it's on my car so good luck trying to get it!!!!

Anyway, we had some down-time, and this older man came up to me. I don't know, maybe in his 80s or late 70s, he wouldn't tell me his age. But he came up and said, "Are you Okay? I see something on your neck." "Oh yeah, I'm fine, just a little hot in the bedroom with my husband." He looked at me with such sincere eyes, and said, "Kristinea, you don't need to do this, everyone knows me around here; I have a lot of money. Let me take care of you for the rest of your life. I promise you that you will never have to worry about anything. Give me my last dying wish. You look like my wife of 65 years of marriage. I met her the same way, well, not really," he said, "but she was a rocket in Vegas. I fell in love at first sight. I lost my wife years ago," he told me, "to cancer." He talked about all the battles they went through together and all the happiness and tears. He had me crying. But he gave me his phone number.

I got done that night, and after I had supper at a soup shop, all Canadian. Damn, it was cold that day -30 below at least! I thought about that old man and what would my Dad say? What about my daughter? What about my husband? I wanted to go with him so bad, but I couldn't. I didn't want to be considered white trash. I still loved my husband, and I just couldn't do that. *I'm sure you're resting at peace now Sir...*he was in the Military. He was in The Navy; he flew

The Story of an Old Centerfold

planes in many wars. He looked pretty good too for his age. Then I thought of my Goddess. I was turning out like her…men at my feet constantly. Gifts, Flowers, Perfume, everything you can think of except up front money.

When I was there, I smoked some weed and holy shit, the dude I was with was like, "Yeah, now you know why I quit. Ha! Ha!" I couldn't wait to get home and see my Brother, Gordy, to tell him about the pot. But anyway, that man never left my mind over the years. What would it have been like if I'd gone with him? Always the what if's I sometimes think about.

I did many other trips and then came Mobile Alabama, close to Panama City, Florida. I realized on this trip, that this whole thing I was doing was nothing but a big drunk fest; rock n roll and sex everywhere I turned. I went to the club in Florida, back when it was MTV, the real MTV. I was at the club in Panama City. My magazine guy was very ill with cancer, and he was still working, so I had another magazine guy there with his wife and a security guard. I meet the owner, Patrick was his name. You think I'm conceited? This man was bragging about how his KISS boots looked and what they cost. He drove a fucking Lamborghini. Anyway, I did my signing session, and I didn't want to go home. So, Glenn, what a sweet man he was, went to bed and I stayed with the other three. I had $500 credit at each bar, arranged by him. The place was entirely wood. Every room you would walk into, there was different music and a bar. There was a pool, and the beach was right over the fence. I was given a box of condoms and was throwing them out to everyone because people were having sex everywhere.

Kristinea

We got wasted and then I was invited to go to his house and party. So, we did. I think the guard was pissed, but hey, I wanted to see what was up at this house. We pull up and I tell you, million-dollar home, pool, hot tub, I don't know how many bedrooms, and oh the nakedness. It was everywhere, not to mention the orgies that were going on in the pool and hot tub. I was scared to go inside the house, but I did. I'd seen my choice of drug, cocaine. Damn right I did some and so did the others. We all just danced all night and talked and drank some more and I went to lay down. I woke up to this fucker right next to me. As I rolled over, he said, " You're in my bed," "Oh My...I got to go." I said, gathering myself. My clothes were still on, and I could tell no one messed with me.

Women, just know, with my mind set on not cheating on the man I love; I wouldn't do it. So, I was supposed to meet Glenn down for breakfast at the hotel at 8:30 am. Well, I was late, he called my boss. "Ha! Ha! We got Kristinea MIA!" he told them. I showed up about 20 minutes late and went right to the table sat down and didn't say a word, except, "I'm sorry for being late." "I had to call The Magazine, first time in 25 years and tell them you were MIA." I laughed so damn hard, stood up and said, "Glenn, you're the best. Thanks for letting me hangout with everyone last night." I gave him a kiss on the cheek. "Yeah, he says, "So did you get into any orgies?" "Hell no," I said. He told me I looked extremely hungover, and I was. Fuck, it was spring break of course I'm going to party it up. I had a radio station interview the next day so I could rest all day and stay in my hotel room and order food service and look out the sliding glass door at the ocean again. So peaceful it was and tranquility.

The Story of an Old Centerfold

I called home a lot, Dad had my daughter again. Nothing but the best for him money, cigs, and booze, Busch Light. So, I made my important calls and went to bed. I didn't hear from the sexy man in the company 'til that night. He called me asking what happened last night. I was scared to tell him, so I told him some things not everything that I'm writing, that's for damn sure. But I could tell there was something bothering him. Me or possibly the office had some drama, or maybe I caused the drama, who knows, who cares, I was okay. I was escorted by a security guard and two magazine distributors, husband, and wife. Now, they hopped right in those damn orgies, that's when I decided to go into the house. I didn't want to watch and had no point in being interested in that shit. He was definitely… different; his voice, laugh, everything… I could tell over the phone. I didn't do anything wrong I told him. I know I had a few more times that I would be seeing him, I said to myself, "Lord, please don't make this man have a crush on me." I prayed . No way could I do that; no way that was my boss. My handsome boss, tanned boss, big handed boss, sexy voice boss, beautiful teeth boss, the list goes on and on with that man. His looks, oh my I still can close my eyes and see him. I had a weakness for this man, a big one.

I thought I hung up the phone. I got my Mr. Bullet out because he was on my mind. Hey, a woman sometimes must do what a woman needs to do. And boy did I do it. Climax after climax and another one. I would touch my body in ways that no one could imagine, because I wanted to live in a fantasy for a while. Then I hear the phone make a noise. It was a busy signal sign. I hung it up and just as I hung it up, the sexy man called in a happy mood. He said, "You know Kristinea, I just heard everything on the phone you were doing." "Oh Shit," I

said. "That was just a relief for me, because of you. You turn me on." "I'm a married woman," I reminded him. He knew. Then he told me he jacked off to my pictures all the time, he told me I was the most beautiful Midwest girl around. I turned him on. "Oh...Okay," I said, shaking like a leaf. You don't want to hear this from your own boss, but then again, I was nude so what else would I expect? It got to the point where I went home again for about two weeks. I was making the money, damn good money too. Mom and Dad continued to watch my daughter. Then we would spend time together and I would leave, I barely saw my husband; he was off making money and I was off making money. I continued to get checks in the mail. I never did mention I wanted to invest again; I didn't want to get beat up. So, I kept my mouth shut, for a long time about that. Never brought it up again.

Chapter 6

I continued my travels, went home and things seemed really different between my husband and me, not seeing each other for months at a time. Things started to calm down. No beatings no fights, just love, like the first time I met him. He was proud of me and didn't really care what anyone thought of me anymore. He had me and that it seemed like it was finally enough for him. It was good times, but I knew I was just a trophy wife, at that point. But it was different for a long time.

My next trip was Las Vegas for the Adult Awards show. Yes, you heard me right the Adult Awards for people in porn and all the above. Oh, my...holy shit. The crap I saw there, you are not going to believe when I tell you. But I was the only Centerfold there.

I got sick because I had my wisdom teeth pulled and they gave me pain pills. I was sicker than a dog. I had to go behind the cover and throw up. My handsome boss was pissed off at me. "What do I have to do to keep an eye on you? Damn it Kristinea, why are you

sick?" I showed him my beautiful teeth and the meds. "WHY?" He told me there was a car on the way to come pick me up. He then said, "Get in the car and go get rest." That is actually what I did. We had to go to the awards show, later that night.

I got some good rest, ate, and didn't touch a penny of liquor. I got ready, did my hair as good as I thought I could, I had on a red dress, with silver glitter on it, two spaghetti straps on the shoulders, and silver glitter high heels on. I didn't look too fucking bad I thought and throughout the night I wasn't the only one that thought that. My Boss called me and told me to come over so we could go together. I said, "Okay, I'll be over."

Two doors away from me, I knocked on the door, he opened it, he looked absolutely handsome in my eyes, and then the words came out of his mouth.

"Oh, Kristinea, please…make a turn for me." I did. He asked me to do it again, but slower, he wanted to see my beauty he told me. I did it, he then invited me in for a drink. What I saw was an open bar, tons of empty, half full, or full, liquor glasses and behind them were or had to be the liquor bottle he was drinking from. I smelled a few of them when he wasn't looking. I had some champagne, in a bucket that looked like gold. I had a few sips, and that's when it started. He began to put his head in my private area, crying about his ex-wife and how she left him for a man that was more successful than him. I tried a few times to lift his head up and it was heavy because he was totally wasted.

Then he began to take his anger out on me, telling me that I had to fuck him, or I would be fired. I said, "Oh no I don't, the voters voted for me not you." My automatic reaction was to be on guard of myself

The Story of an Old Centerfold

and my surroundings. He then told me he was in the mafia, and he would have me killed if I didn't fuck him. That's when I turned around and said, "Okay, here ya go. Ya want to Fuck me, here I'm right here." I began to take off my double spaghetti strap dress, one strap at a time, very slowly, looking at him in the eye and telling him, "My Father knows where I am, he knows who I am with, He knows everything."

I then put my heel up on the table and when I did it, the noise made him jump. I began to take it off and try to seduce him with my eyes. As I was taking off one of my shoes, half dressed, I told him, "Ya know My Dad is a tough man, Vietnam Vet, still in contact with his platoon to this day. You touch me, he will find you and I will sue your ass quicker than you know." Then he came up to me and put his hands on me and told me he was sorry. He lifted my straps, and I did my heel while he helped me up front, with what I started to take off anyway. We left and headed downstairs with his arm on mine. I hated the man from that day on. I never looked at him the same. Never and to this day. I want to thank whoever was with me that day, I knew I had an angel watching over me and I was hoping that me telling him about My Dad would scare the shit out of him.

We walked into the Awards, I sat with six people that night. A woman big in porn, her parents, someone else, my boss and me. There was amazing food and silver-plated tables all around filled with booze. You could just walk up and fill your glass. I noticed and so did my boss, this man was coming up, smelling the wine cart next to our table. He would smell it, swirl it around, put his pinky finger it in and taste it and look at me, then he started throughout the evening to do this over and over and then he pointed at me.

My boss noticed, he stood up went over there and asked him if he needed anything because I could hear it, that's how close he was to our cart. He came up and introduced himself and said he was a porn director and he wanted me. He offered me $350K for three movies. My boss got out his fancy ass cigar and interrupted him asking for a light. He began to talk some more; honestly, it was going through one ear and out the other. I told him "I'm very flattered that you asked me that sir, but I do have morals and My Dad would kick my ass, right boss?" That was it. He grabbed me by the arm, very hard I may say, and said, "Kristinea, I can't take you anywhere without something or someone coming up to you. I'm sick of it." I pulled away my arm so quick and said, "I get this shit at home; I'm not getting it here!"

There was a sign that said if you left you couldn't get back in. We got in the limo, and I poured me a big shot of vodka, the expensive kind. I sat back and realized this shit isn't all fun and games or glitz and glamor it felt like sometimes, but deep down it wasn't. It kinda shocked me, just everything that happened. We arrived at the Hard Rock Cafe in Vegas where we were staying. He told me to go get dressed in regular clothing and meet him down at the craps table. "Yeah, whatever," I thought. I did what he asked, walked down and he was there with a woman that had fake tits and was he hitting on her. I got lost in the crowd and watched George Thorogood in concert that night. I charged everything up on that damn card. The reason why is because all the bullshit I had put up with that night. *Yeah, I'm going to pay you back asshole.* Ha! Ha! And I know he was making a lot of fucking money off me. So, that's what I did. Bought some people some drinks and rocked the night away.

The Story of an Old Centerfold

    I was happy with who I was, and I stood up for myself. I sure the hell wasn't going to be a pin up girl on his wall of fuck buddies. I went to bed drunk off my ass and had to wake up early and do a radio show. That was a lot of fun, good people. I wore a black pair of hippie-like pants with a "Got Milk" shirt on and hat. My Dad gave me the hat and I had the shirt. They got a kick out of that. I went home after about 4 days of signing books, pictures, radio interview and of course the show.

But the last night I was there I was dragged to a Sushi Party invitation only. I was told I had to stay the whole time by my boss. I said, "Okay." We show up to a huge ass room and a table. On that table a beautiful woman, didn't know who she was but, in my eyes, she was absolutely gorgeous. She was covered in vegetables, fruit, and sushi of all damn things. Anyway, the night went on and we were all wasted. I think there was about 20 people there. I then began to see the men eat off this woman. She didn't seem to mind, so I just watched. I heard the moans and groans and kinda got turned on. Money being thrown at her like crazy. You could not go down under the waist. But they broke the rules anyway and was going down on her. I looked at her and her eyes told me something. I'd seen stretch marks on the side of her legs, I then knew she had a child. Or maybe a couple, she was doing this for money and money only, and I understood. I really understood. The guys were getting rough and feisty. I was the only woman there. My boss whispered in my ear, "So are you going to take a bite or you just going to sit there?" "How much money are you willing to give her if I do this?" I asked him. He told me, "Hundreds." I said, "Prove it." He opened his wallet and there was a stack of one-hundred-dollar bills. I said, "Okay. I see in her eyes what she is going through though." "No, Kristinea, she does this for a living." He spoke. "No, you don't understand what I'm saying." I replied. I did it. I got on the table in a beautiful outfit; I got on her and ate off her boobs, I didn't go below the waist. The men were throwing money at her and me like crazy. It was like the old days, but it didn't last long. I got done in about five minutes.

I sat back down and told my boss give her the money, NOW. He did, five hundred in total. I began to leave, I told him I was tired and

The Story of an Old Centerfold

drunk and just want to go home. He said, "Okay, I'm staying, have fun." But before I walked away from the little connection I had with this woman, I whispered in her ear, "I hope this helps you." She said thank you, as I could see somewhat a tear come down her face . I never saw her again, but I knew she could see me, and I could see her, and we were connecting with our eyes, we were telling our story by looking at each other with eye contact. Sometimes those are the best, and sometimes they are not.

    I finally made it home. I did more travels and went to my last one, in Atlantic City. It was *Perfect 10 Girls of the Year* and I, The *Girl of the Year*. I arrive there and I had an escort that was a fucking bitch to me. Bigtime bitch. We had a line of men going out, I don't know how long, out of the door. Some of them want to just talk for a few. I was at the end. Best for last, I guess. HA! Anyway, I was running out of pictures and magazines. I asked the escort if she could please grab me some, "That's your job," she told me. I said, "Excuse me? I'm supposed to sit here and look pretty, smile and meet men that want to meet me, I'm not getting up from this chair." She said, "Oh yes you are." And then I said to myself, "This is MY LAST DAY. I've been paid in full." I stood up and told that fucking bitch, after I grabbed my black and whites, "Is your name Kristinea?" "No," she said. I said, "It is now." I threw that shit at her and walked out. I walked the fuck out of there. I had had enough.

    It was taking a toll on me, I was drunk all the time, I was tired all the time, I was just done with the bullshit. I called and told them what happened and told a lie; that my Bitch of a husband got hurt on the job, I had to go home early anyway. With that being said, I was done. I do wish that my last trip would have been better but sometimes ya

Kristinea

know the old saying, *you can't always get what you want.* I walked away, I did my job, I was successful at it and that was the end of my career with that company. *I would like to say to all of you thank you for that. It is a part of my life. Ninety percent of the time I enjoyed myself and for that, I thank you.* I did speak to them one time after I was finished, and they had all the magazines there and pictures. I asked what they were going to do with them. They told me they were going to shred them…I said, "No! I will pay for all the shipping send them to me, I want them all."

Chapter 7

I was done with this company for real and I was happy, I went and cut my hair, never again will I do that. HA! I felt so damn free from all the shit. I was getting along with my husband, and we got rid of the lake house. I traveled with my husband, bad idea. Real bad idea. The beatings continued but included my hair this time, a lot of my hair. Just doing laundry, cooking for the crew, and being a mother. Well, we got into cocaine bad. Really bad. He beat me, forced me again to have sex with his boss so he didn't get fired. Again, he got the sloppy seconds. And he beat my daughter worse. I don't know who got it worse her or me.

He would always hide everything from me. My keys, my wallet, my debit card, everything you can imagine. I was stuck out on the east coast when 9/11 happened. He tried to kidnap my daughter one night. I had to scream for help at a gas station so he wouldn't take her from me. It got to the point where it was supper time with about 3-9 men per day. I cooked supper all the time. He would call and tell me

that hey I got this person coming and a few others. I cooked my ass off. That's when it got ugly.

    He used to make me tell all his coworkers, "Tell them what's going to happen to you, if you cheat on me babe," I had to say, "He has told me he will put me in the woodchipper, feet first, alive and get away with it because of his position with the company and his father." I had to fucking say that to his buddies, what bullshit. Years later we had a little girl...*sorry sweetheart you're named after a stripper, and it is not your mother's name.* Just being honest.

    I finally got to the point where I could leave. We got into crack so bad, we were spending over $2K a month on it. One night, he went for a drug run. I looked everywhere for anything that could get me out of this trap and cage I felt I was in. I finally found my wallet and car keys. I decided that night, I was done. Done with the drugs, done with the beatings, just fucking done. I left him. He damaged my heart that's for sure, again. I was done; I threw away all the drug paraphernalia. I'M THE ONE THAT THREW IT AWAY. I tried to call him when I got to Pennsylvania, no answer, tried again, no answer. I knew right then my marriage was done.

    I came home, of course to My Dad's. I was a wreck, I didn't have withdrawals though, I got away from that drug and that was that; I got away from an evil man and that was that. My father always being my savior, helped me out a lot and my daughter. Down on your luck, need a few bucks, I'm here Bean. Need someone to talk to? I'm here Bean. Need a friend and Father, I am here Bean. He was, more than my Mother. Don't get me wrong, I love My Mom, but things where so different with my Dad and me. As I write this, I can remember who could drink who under the table....Always ME! That's not something

The Story of an Old Centerfold

to be proud of. But that was my Father and I, always together when we needed one another. I paid his bills for a few months because I had the money to do so, well....not no more. I had him in my life for 36 years and I'm okay with that, as I sit here, I write on the computer he bought me 11 years ago.

I finally got my shit somewhat together and moved to Illinois. I was attending college, top notch community college. You had to be the best of the best or you were screwed, good grades or nothing, you would receive nothing. I did okay in nursing; my favorite was English papers. But I failed one class. I was going to repeat it in the summer of 2010.

Then I got the call. My Dad was very ill, due to Agent Orange cancer in his brain, lungs, and lymph nodes. I called him, he had GERD (acid reflex) so bad, he couldn't even talk without spitting up, what I found out later was tar on a towel. I told him I was coming home. He told me, "No Bean, do your classes and come home after that."

"No way, no way Dad, I'm coming home." I was my Dad's 100 percent caregiver and I worked graveyard shift as a CNA, two jobs I had. We wouldn't have made it, if, it wasn't for his VA Benefits. I was thankful for that, and my Dad always told me, "Bean, I have all this money now, and I'm dying." It was hard to take from such a strong Marine, wise, wonderful man, and handsome I may add, he looked like Clint Eastwood to me. I was losing my father, my Dad, and my best friend. Superbowl Sunday at 1:06 am I lost my Dad. I hugged him for so long and cried my damn eyes out, I still do. The last thing I said to him was, "Dad you're going to Paradise." They say hearing is the last thing that goes, I wanted him to know I was there. I was. As I write this, I still cry for him. I couldn't grieve for my Dad for many reasons.

Kristinea

My Dad knew I met a man online. No Secret. I didn't want to be alone after my Dad passed away. I dated this man for about 10 months. He also lied to me about his name. He went by his middle name, not his first name. Dad just knew I had a friend. He was okay with it; I told him why. I hugged him months before and said, "Dad what am I going to do when you are gone?" He told me, "Bean, you're going to be okay sweetheart," as he hugged me so tight and loving and so ill. I believed him. I wasn't okay. Two months before he passed away, I finally asked my Dad, "Why did you nickname me Bean Dad?" He said, "Shit Bean, you used to eat green beans out of style when you were younger; like crazy." I finally knew why after all these years. I still eat them, but with cheese. The man I was seeing helped me take care of my Father. He would sit there and watch football games with him while I was sleeping or when I had to leave to go to work at ten. My Father passed away in February of 2011.

Three months later after my Father passed (*and a year to the day my Father had been diagnosed with cancer everywhere in his body*) May 14th, 2011, I decided to go to a carnival with the man I was still seeing. I hadn't been there since I was a teenager, about 17 years old. It was a well-attended carnival celebrating a Czech tradition in our town. Mom watched my daughter and told me to be home by 8PM.

We went with a friend of his, his sister, and her friend. I looked good that night. I was strutting it; I lost a lot of weight and I put on makeup.

The Story of an Old Centerfold

We were arguing before we even got to our destination.

Chapter 8

"Kristinea, Kristinea, wake up honey. Do you know where you are?" All I knew is that my head was killing me. I asked for something for my head. I went right back to sleep. I don't remember much. The three main things I remember, is a private investigator and a sheriff, coming to speak to me. I found out somewhat what had happened to me. I was told I was physically assaulted by the P.O.S (piece of shit) man, I was seeing, and I had bleeding and bruising on both sides of my head.

All I wanted at that point was my Marine, my Dad. I also remember a very bright light, a long rectangular door, and smoke it looked like, or fluffy clouds. I tried to convince myself it was the ER doctor going through the doors. But it wasn't. My Father was behind me in regular clothes and leaning down praying for me with his hands crossed. Then I saw him get up and walk into the light, his clothes changing into his Marine outfit; there is a Heaven, and my Dad was there. I think he saved my life and God; it wasn't my time. My husband now, that

The Story of an Old Centerfold

I've been with or known for 11 years this year is the one that took care of me; he and my mother. I couldn't write, shower, eat, talk, walk, everything you can imagine when taking care of a toddler. I had to relearn everything over, and I mean everything. I was in a coma for 5 days and the hospital for about two weeks. My husband and I were friends at the time this happened, he was there with me, every night at the hospital.

After I got home, I barely remembered my home that I'd counted on for over 15 years, and the kitchen chair was empty. I remember watching my Dad's DVD of all the pictures and songs we all picked out for his service and cried for about two weeks. Then I thought to myself, "Wait a minute, this P.O.S did this to me after my Father died and he would sit with him when he was alive? *You, if you are reading this you know who you are, I can't wait 'til you see my Dad again; you may not get in.* After all, my Dad couldn't hurt a damn flea, but he was dying. *I know that if he were alive, he would have killed you and went to jail for it. What does a sick Marine have to lose, but everything to gain by making sure you are 6 feet under. So have fun with that when YOUR day comes.*

My brother stopped by to see me, after I got home, and he saw a somewhat older man taking care of me in my father's and my home. I told him, "Don't be mad, I need help G, I need help."

I didn't see my brother too much after that. We both lived different lives and lifestyles. For three years of my life, it was an absolute fog. I don't remember much. I was on everything possible medication wise, and I went through every therapy you could imagine. I finally got somewhat normal and tried to spend time with all my daughters; three of them, by three different men. Yeah, some may call me

a whore or a slut, but I don't care. I lived this life. As far as the bitch goes, well, we don't talk anymore, I call him that because when we would argue he would call me an asshole. *Well, okay you are a fucking bitch.* I haven't seen my youngest daughter for several years. I had no more money to fight him. I will say this, *"YOUR day will come as well, just like everyone else."* If you are a parent, you don't push to brain wash your child/children to hate the other parent. It's not right, and it will affect them when they get older. I forgot how old she is now but, if you are reading this my young one, *I miss you. This is my story and it's the truth. I don't know how long they keep records of domestic abuse, but he did it to me and your sister. I hope you believe me, because it is the truth of everything that I went through with him and yes, that was your Mom on the poster in the room. I remember all the stories you used to tell me young one, and the rest is history. Now you know everything you need to know.*

As far as my other two girls they are grown now and have told me to go to hell, rot in hell, everything you can imagine, I've heard it all. I'm okay with it. I'm just a dog mom anyway. My oldest daughter, I am not happy with the way she turned out, but that's on her. I really have nothing else I want to say about it. Except, she knows the truth about The Bitch, she just blames me. Now, we have a lot of hate towards each other. I hope this someday too, shall pass not just with her but with all my girls. I'm not a bad Mom and I'm not a good Mom either.

All I can say to all three of you is, *"I apologize, for not being around when you needed me. I was too busy putting myself first, and not my children. I know we have had our arguments that escalate to pure evil words and harassment. I'm done now with all of that, I'll never stop*

The Story of an Old Centerfold

loving all three of you, but I'm not a doormat anymore, I'm not a bag of potatoes you can just throw wherever you want; you respect your elders. Yes, I have done wrong, I have told whoever decides to read this all my sins. It's not an easy thing to do.......but it's been one hell of a ride, writing this."

I am happily married now, for almost six years coming up in August. I am treated like a queen, and I don't get beat on. He loves my kids even though they don't come around anymore.

To my Mom I say, *"I love you. I'm thankful you are still here with us. I know you lost a child, my brother, G, three years after Dad, but know that I am sorry for all the hell I put you through growing up. I know was a handful and still am. But You are one strong woman, Mom, I'm thankful for you."*

I can't hold down a job due to my TBI (traumatic brain injury) because I take THC pills and sometimes, I smoke it. I worked with the elderly for over 15 years. It was my medicine for what that P.O.S did to me. I worked with the elderly, and I finally had enough of it. I put those clothes up in the closet and I don't look at them much anymore. I will never forget a few people I took care of, especially My Dad. My Mom was also there to help; I consider myself blessed. I got to see my parents fall in love again after 40 years of divorcing each other.

I am now at the end of my story. My Life. I am going to be 46 years old here soon, I should have done this sooner, but I wasn't ready. I am speaking up now. I'm always going to be me, always remember where I come from, and *yeah Dad, my boots are on.* I still drink, yeah and I smoke pot due to my injury; it's my medicine for all the damn headaches I continue to have, due to that P.O.S. who put me in the hospital.

I began to have seizures shortly before writing this book… and they can't find anything wrong with me, but it is from the brain injury.

I want to tell the state of Iowa to, "Kiss my black widow ass." I'm permanently damaged by that man's bad actions. The only thing that P.O.S gave me, was I got to see my Father again and I am content with that. I did feel I was abandoned by whoever took the assault case back in 2011. *You owe me a service dog…if not that, an apology at least would be nice.* Maybe I deserved what I got. *Whoever called 911 that day, thank you…*I don't know how long I was unconscious on the ground. To my knowledge that P.O.S only served a day or two in jail. I didn't get shit for help; had no job due to taking time off work to grieve my Dad. No victim assistance, nothing. It's not easy to move on now and forgive when I am living with the physical disabilities, but I must. Nothing was or can be done for justice to be served; only to tell my story.

My last words in this book…*Yes state of Iowa, you can kiss my black widow ass.*

Like I said, "It's Been One Hell of a Ride…."

Love,
Kristinea

Endnotes

For those who made it through my story, please don't judge.

Due to my traumatic brain injury, my grammar may be wrong; please forgive me for that.

If I can keep a young girl out of this industry and from doing what I did years ago, then I've done my job.

Peace Out!

Dirty Laundry
VooDoo
People Are Strange
Rooster

www.ingramcontent.com/pod-product-compliance
Ingram Content Group UK Ltd.
Pitfield, Milton Keynes, MK11 3LW, UK
UKHW022241230426
12048UKWH00018BA/1386